A Place Comfortable with Fire

A Place Comfortable with Fire

John Milkereit

LITERARY PRESS
LAMAR UNIVERSITY

ISBN: 978-1-942956-57-0
Library of Congress Control Number: 2022949373

Cover photo credit: Varsha Saraiya-Shah

Lamar University Literary Press
Beaumont, Texas

For the gentle reader seeking fire

Other poetry from Lamar University Literary Press

Lisa Adams, *xuāi: mission, house, village, town*
Bobby Aldridge, *An Affair of the Stilled Heart*
Michael Baldwin, *Lone Star Heart, Poems of a Life in Texas*
Charles Behlen, *Failing Heaven*
David Bowles, *Flower, Song, Dance: Aztec and Mayan Poetry*
Jerry Bradley, *Collapsing into Possibility*
Jerry Bradley, *Crownfeathers and Effigies*
Jerry Bradley and Urf Kirchdorfer, *The Great American Wise Ass Poetry Anthology*
Matthew Brennan, *One Life*
Matthew Brennan, *Snow in New York*
Mark Busby, *Through Our Times*
Julie Chappell, *Mad Habits of a Life*
Stan Crawford, *Resisting Gravity*
Chip Dameron and Betsy Joseph, *Relatively Speaking*
Chip Dameron, *Waiting for an Etcher*
Glover Davis, *Academy of Dreams*
Jeffrey DeLotto, *Voices Writ in Sand*
Chris Ellery, *Elder Tree*
Dede Fox, *On Wings of Silence*
Larry Griffin, *Cedar Plums*
Lynn Hoggard, *First Light, Poems of Love and Loss*
Michael Jennings, *Crossings, a Record of Travel*
Gretchen Johnson, *A Trip Through Downer, Minnesota*
Markham Johnson, *Dear Dreamland*
Betsy Joseph, *Only So Many Autumns*
Ulf Kirchdorfer, *Chewing Green Leaves*
Laozi, *Daodejing*, translated by David Breeden, Steven Schroeder, and Wally Swist
Laurence Musgrove, *Local Bird*
Benjamin Myers, *Black Sunday*
Godspower Oboido, *Wandering Feet on Pebbled Shores*
Dave Oliphant, *The Pilgrimage, Selected Poems: 1962-2012*
Kornelijus Platelis, *Solitary Architectures*
Carol Coffee Reposa, *Underground Musicians*
Jan Seale, *A Lifetime of Words*
Jan Seale, *The Parkinson Poems*
Steven Schroeder, *the moon, not the finger, pointing*
Vincent Spina, *The Sumptuous Hills of Gulfport*
W. K. Stratton, *Ranchero Ford/Dying in Red Dirt Country*
Gary Swaim, *Quixotic Notions*
Ken Waldman, *Sports Page*
Loretta Diane Walker, *Ode to My Mother's Voice*
Dan Williams, *Past Purgatory, a Distant Paradise*
Jonas Zdanys, *The Angled Road*
Jonas Zdanys, *Three White Horses*

For information on these and other Lamar University Literary Press books:
https://www.lamar.edu/literary-press/

Acknowledgments

I am grateful to the editors of the following journals, chapbooks, and anthologies in which some of these poems first appeared:

Abandoned Mine
Civilized Beasts
di-verse-city: An Anthology of the Austin International Poetry Festival
Weaving the Terrain: 100-Word Southwestern Poems,
    Dos Gatos Press
Harbinger Asylum
Odes and Elegies: Eco-Poetry from the Texas Gulf Coast,
    Lamar University Literary Press
Unlocking the Word: An Anthology of Found Poetry,
    Lamar University Literary Press
Echoes of the Cordillera,
    Museum of the Big Bend, Sul Ross State University
Enchantment of the Ordinary,
    Mutabilis Press
Panoply
Paying Admissions and *Home & Away,*
    Pudding House Press
San Pedro River Review
Texas Poetry Calendar
The Ekphrastic Review
The Ocotillo Review
Quiet Diamonds 2020,
    The Orchard Street Press

Sarah Cortez made a huge contribution to the organization of this collection. Chelsey Clammer made valuable editorial comments on the manuscript. Sandi Stromberg was gracious enough to proofread the work on multiple occasions. Any mistakes are mine.

Poets in the Loop is my monthly critique group where many of these poems were initially workshopped. Thank you, Dom, Winston, Chuck, Mary, Elina, Kelly, Vanessa, Varsha, and Carrie. Participants of the San Miguel Poetry Week also saw some of this work and made it better.

CONTENTS

In Bright Shock

Wearing You like a Gas Mask

Drowning in Art

Drinking the Troubled Milk

In Bright Shock

Cry Joy Park—Why Are You Dark and Light?
   after Jennifer Wen Ma's installation,
   Cry Joy Park—Gardens of Dark and Light

Because I sour
your vinegar is sweet.

Because I corrode
and your palm oil is not rust.

Because I am bland
and you, your sharp peppers—

   Would you ever
   say a prayer for me?

My ink, a swirl of metal.
My water, rivulets.

Favor me into your skin.
Lick my salt.

Honey is the first taste.
Your pleasure. Sweet.

Can I drink that Barbados rum
the bottle shining on your table?

Sit in my wooden chair to eat
kola nuts for bitter.

Pluck my black and white leaves.
My garden will feed you.

   I took you in darkness,
   I reach you in bright shock.

The Night You Can't See

You can't see what's inside the night.
Possums and almost running over your neighbor's dog,
sleepwalking in the snow,
whoever pierced the kitchen window with BB shots.

The wine train to Napa but no vines to see.
You didn't see hash browns that scattered, smothered,
and covered what sloshed in your stomach.
You didn't see a woman's desire to sit in your lap
at the blues bar after you offered her the last seat.

You've forgotten that it isn't easy
drinking at Blind Willies.
You didn't see holiday lights in the pear tree.
Varsity runs started all-nighters.
You never saw that coming.
Or the pigeon wearing an onion ring necklace.

It's better to practice saying the alphabet backward
before a cop stops you.
You did see yourself almost veer
into a lamppost after switching lanes
at the intersection on Orange Blossom Trail.

No way to see if you can touch your nose
with your eyes closed. Seeing beauty at night
might be the early stage of warped love.
You never saw your father roam the park as a vampire.
You can see playing cards better in the morning.

At the Charleston Naval Shipyard

I stenciled changes to submarine tenders

with black pens on a drafting board,

showing revised centers of gravity.

My neck was choked by a polka-dotted tie,

bought cheap on King Street. I drove a blue Ford Pinto

hatchback with a faulty fuel tank. Brake lines

hid trapped air like a dark velvet curtain before I

rear-ended a car. I felt raw, a crash in sulfur air

as the coast became crumpled metal dressed as salt.

I was nineteen. After my stint ended, I rode Greyhound

back to Atlanta for college, and fell in love for the first time

with Nancy, a woman waiting in line for football tickets,

her shoulders, two hushed magnolia petals. How could I know

love could begin by meeting a woman majoring in chemistry

by standing on a sidewalk, my internals thrown into cautious yellow,

my center eventually sank for months with mono?

How did she know to stand in front, that she would catch

a regular man off balance?

Pluto

I read your mystery, in the newspaper,
distant, tiny, elliptical, orbiting
the star from where we are every 248 years.
You excelled past theory, drove
February nights, images over northern Arizona;
generations memorized solar system charts.
Your weightiness, spherical good nature
never did you in—you would not slingshot
past the neighborhood. Your lock
with your companion, Charon, revoked
planetary status as facts known
many calendars before my existence—
black and white—they change
with discovery, icy evidence
beyond the belt of what is known unfolds...
weaponry from spider webs, blind deer hunters...
how the bodies of reason and moderation,
matters that spun Aristotle's mind elongate
to this plane. Years ago, I met a woman
who skewed my atmosphere upside down,
freezing space I knew as unexplainable.
The launch to horizons unknown
was the furthest journey we took until separation.
Those fractures broke boundaries after meeting
only hours before, and as far away as three city blocks—
traveling the same direction—until our paths
collided in a traffic accident. We saw contrasts
of light and dark pressed into cracks of glass.

The Occasionally Passionate Shepherd of Love Apocalypse

Move in with me and be my love apocalyptically.

The way I feel about a duck walking into a bar—
asks the bartender for duck food—I'm often
very emotional depending on the bartender's response.
If a duck is fed, the world is in harmony.

If not, I would take the duck in, and find some food
on the threat of her webbed feet being nailed to the bar.

I am not saying the duck lives with me forever.
I could fill a small plastic pool of water so she could swim.
But I would find cleaning the pool a hassle. I hate cleaning.

Didn't the Mayans say the world would end on January 1st, 2000?
Months before, I was passionate about Janet. But eventually,
we had issues, such as, "You need to slow down on the freeway,"
and "You need to accept that Andy is going to bark the whole way."

Andy was her dog, and I was driving while he barked
close to my ear like I was headed for road rage
at Janet's parents' house, which was incorrect. I did not
passionately love Andy, but that Thanksgiving was quiet
at Janet's parents' house, even though I was not madly in love
with the White Zinfandel, which tasted like vinegar.

When the Mayans screwed up, I became more intermittently passionate.

But today, after taking a thoughtful inventory of my feelings
for Janet, my passionate love has rekindled. Andy barks
in dog heaven, and I sip the health benefits of vinegar.

I would gladly accept eating ham again at the Golden Corral
in Splendora, especially after Easter service
sitting on the football stadium bleachers.

In God's final judgment, the bar closed.
No more ducks. I am cleansed of beer, and I like cleaning.
Now that I am more passionately available,
go ahead, move in with me and be my endless love.

The Erotica Inside Me Does Not Quiet
after Toyen's painting, *Potato Theatre*

like an alarm clock that keeps melting
but never stops. The sea is gentle enough

to dance with you, even though
hairs on my only leg do not find

much tide, or is it the calm before
we are assassinated by war?

We did not deserve this pleasure as if
we found both halves of unmated wolves.

Yet I am not a predator. Behind this suit
I masquerade more like a clown.

When your wet hip invades my hip,
we wade in the sound of a saxophone.

Hands float across a piano, and the wind
begins a tender assault. I smell

the sex of you. Underneath your hat
is vanilla followed by salt, which is somehow

dusted off at your neck by cinnamon. No,
not wolves. Instead, my body is a funny potato

with less skin, and you blossom like a grapefruit
split open. I want to sip a little bit of your juice,

maybe commit enough sin to curl your toes.
Love is the only thing to be killed by.

We are pawns of this light that melts us,
and the theatre must go on and on...

I Am Not Writing about the Rose,
I Am Making It Bloom in the Paper

I replace the ink from the pen with water.
I tear bits of paper from the corners for dirt.
I cannot wait until spring. I have been told to make
       this rose blossom now like in January.
If I do not start now, the rose will die.
I tell the bare root that I love you for yourself
       like telling a child on the first day of school.
I will prick myself to get the rose's attention,
       blood if necessary since I have too much.
I have plenty to offer.
I squirt water when the paper is dry.
I sleep when the rose wants to sleep.
I whisper an offer to live with me near a good window.
I eat dinner with the rose.
I cup my hands into a mad contortion to show the rose
       what two blossoms look like.
I smile more now.
The jokes about roses I keep to myself.
I whisper something sweet.
I make more dirt so the rose will keep standing.
I crease the edges, so it knows where to grow.

Traveling on Fire

At the airport this afternoon,
the security agent with a bun on his head
wore a navy shirt with "Hamilton" written
in block letters.

As the smoke-eyed woman inspected
backpacks, the conveyor belt whirled.
She shook her head when asked about belts and shoes.

In the boarding area, another woman revealed
a raging puppet with a black hat who sang
"Amazing Grace." She found a volunteer to lip
sync "God Bless America" only she lit a match
and flames erupted from the volunteer's lips.

And a girl in her pink ballerina outfit twirled
around with her backpack until she escaped
her mother, crying until a stuffed monkey arrived.

This is how the journey began.
The airplane soared from the middle coast to Reno
as I sat at the window near the wing

with passengers reading electrons
from their electronic tablets or playing video
games. The pen had nothing shocking

to say. My notebook never lit up. Armed with
drink coupons, I felt like saying, "Hey,
I want a Bloody Mary," or I would ask loudly,
"I have extra drink coupons, would anyone like one?"

That's how I wanted to break the ice.
Passengers loosening up, alcohol running
down the aisle. Would anyone hear me?

I was almost positive that the ballerina girl
wanted to ask about my day job and my never-ending
love of juggling spreadsheets overlooking the freeway,

which I would have explained as surely as Tarzan would
have slung words from a vine to describe the jungle. She would
need to open my sliding glass door with her wand to listen.

Desperado

Do not despair. Instead, dance blind to
a Thomas Dolby tune on Peachtree Street asphalt,
or at the Limelight, wheel under a crystal ball.
After midnight, Disco Kroger, drunk off

our chemistry, mac and cheese boxes were thrown
like footballs. French bread drumsticks
on a shopping cart handlebar. The ends
of aisles heartache. Songs we have danced

for as long as we can. We floated sensible
and nonsense, thousands of miles, thousands of sung
and not sung. The scratched record. The needle
that keeps saying this is this, is this.

Christmas in England

I'll fly to Gatwick
romp to Oxford
visit my parents
who left in June

I'll run beside canals
swim with white geese
photo the narrow boats
drink beer with Tolkien

I'll bus to London
paint foggy bridges
theater Piccadilly Square
ride the Circle line

I'll find my stocking
bake yeasted bread
buy holiday books
vacuum-seal winter clothes

And I'll carry on the plane
my eggnog latte launcher
and pack my cavity-fighting
fluorinated detonation

Golden Shovel: Remembering
after Billy Collins

Since you brought it
up, the elevator in my brain has
no lift. Fishing cabins haven't floated
away. Phones still don't take coins in the way
we're used to. I will jot down
the plot, the author, the title in a
notebook with dark
ink that would bleed to mythological
proportions if needed, a river,
a lake, or a sea—it doesn't matter whose
body, their name is just a name.
Where memory begins
is on your tongue, not with
the spleen, definitely not some obscure corner of the spleen, an
organ that lives in a lost city under the *L*
train. I will never forget how to swim as
badly as I tried to Rollerblade. The training wheels I kissed far
enough away as
I remember. The date of the famous war battle you
wanted is mounted on a rocket launched to Mars. Moths can
fly from a love poem, I recall, like silver jets.

You Put a Spell on Me

like a punching bag
hanging off a hardwood floor.
I endure the repeated abuse
of love in this parlor game of travel.
The New Orleans train,
the *Sunset Limited*, is hocus-pocus.
You punch and sprinkle fairy dust
in my all-good-things-lounge-car drink.
You draw from the deck the right playing card.
Heck, inside you know all the tricks.
I try the cabin escape when you bust
out the wand. I bathroom dance
pissing in four mirror angles. I twist
around enough to break from the straps
screwed into the ceiling. We break up
after I fall.

Janus

After the year is over, you begin
again whether we like it,
your entrance overlooking pipes
or across windows unreadied
and clouded, after rosemary
served as a holiday shrub
remembered its roots
when we reminisced where
we had been, writing thank-yous
to no tomorrows to slow the past,
and ease forgetfulness. If we ever
thought of this year, the future,
we'd cringe as though we quiver
against shivered poles,
checking our resolutions,
some downpour on acid soil.

The look ahead, we call for you
since there are no more engagements
while we gather the quilt from the leather sofa
near the fireplace, which startled you then,
or when your voice whispers
a week of joyous warmth,
outbursts that we don't know why
we deserve. You forecast
all the outcomes. We loosen our tongues,
wait. Our roofs open.

Wholeness

after seeing Rodrigo Valenzuela's video, *Diamond Box*

To know wholeness
open a diamond box,
fit yourself inside for the future
like a tool ready for the first work.
What you carry and rely upon,
the food, the bags of shoes, and gallons of water
is never enough,
though all this counts toward
the deception of a journey in the land of wholeness.
How night cloaks your walk
and readies itself like a hotel,
a bed vacancy made of stones and branches,
no walls, not quite so dark under
the pledge of moonshine.

To know the full impact of wholeness,
start over again after one failed attempt.
You must certify this new plan is idiotic and reckless,
which may include a split from the pack after
the police invade.
You must see bones and crosses in the desert.
You need to ready yourself when your toenails
pop off after the removal of your socks.
You know you've arrived when wholeness presses
your hand against these walls turned sideways,
which now feels more like bridges. Your hand
never wants to let go.

Bicyclists

I want to say something in awe
of bicyclists in Houston who believe themselves
immortal. Immortality has legs

that churn radiance
propelling bent-over bodies through jasmine air,
arms extended to prevent slipping over a cliff.

I admire bicyclists who leave
cars in garages to fill
water bottles and welcome danger,

gripping a day like today, Easter, with gloves.
They steer skinny tires away from broken glass,
a narrow path, thread fed to a bad needle head.

And the next day, again.
That's why I want to say something in amazement
like: *When you take the road,*

in lights of reflector and layers of Lycra,
head domed with helmet, buns on a tiny seat,
our hearts suspend

hungry to leap over a trapeze wire
flying across the cables of bridges
soaking up the deep blueness of the afternoon,

the first robin song, the cruise past wine drinkers
on a patio, and now our hearts
are dark crimson comets stabbing the rib cavity.

We have to yearn for adventure,
remember the balance of bicyclists
who forgive injuries, ache in bright suits.

We need to drink their pH-enhanced
water and pedal past the false security
of cars' metal armor.

We have to unlock our cautious faith
and resurrect ourselves
unbolted and elated.

Wearing You like a Gas Mask

What Comes Next
after Dale Patterson's painting, *Beyond the Storm*

is watching the yellow fog
from the nearby beach, so near

more like a mist wave,
a slender horizon, silence caught

enough to divert attention
to the dragonfish with fluttering wings

in marigold, turquoise, and emerald bay.
What comes next are bands of the eye

ready to strip the row house ground
or the roof etched in magenta.

Watch for desire, the sweet treachery
of brandy stains, the insides bat like.

Here's a good idea: find the emergency kit
with five days of packed sardines buried

in the undertow of shadows. Build a hope fire
of driftwood dragged to shore and breathed into.

Search for blown-out copal incense
bought off a cobbled street.

A storm warning came—
greyness,

a new sky, even now,
above and ready to descend.

Danger for June

That was the month Luka Magnotta fled
from Montreal, caught in a Berlin Internet café,
his lover an engineering student ice picked

to pieces on the Internet. It was the month
a woman yellowed a burglar with a paintball gun
who tried to steal her coins and Ramen noodles.

That month a university evaluated the nature of
a suspect, said he didn't pose a threat,
then days later he knifed away the heart and brain,

maybe like he did to another man before,
like flames under smoke, who was hit with a baseball bat
wrapped in chains and barbed wire. Instead of praying

that month, I zoned out with a movie prequel
about a woman scientist who reminded me of Sigourney Weaver,
when an alien impregnated her. Abraham Lincoln

became a vampire hunter in 3D, and I read an ad about the Rejuvenique
Facial Toning Mask that zapped your face with electricity
to feel young again. It was the month I wanted to become a musician

after I saw an interview with a famous cellist, whose
first cello was a toy made from a Rice Krispies cereal box, a chopstick,
and a toothpick, who said her final note was her final breath,

and I wanted to become an actor after seeing a monologue
about Steve Jobs and a factory in Shenzhen, China, that lifted up
nets on buildings to prevent suicides. That month I remember

wanting a woman who fed me brownies laced with weed.
She was covered in fishnet hose, very Gothic looking for a German
heavy metal concert after meeting at Coyote Ugly where I wanted

another woman named Megan, who danced on the bar portrayed in
that movie, whom I bought a Jack Daniels T-shirt if she promised
to scissor it, but she never did. I wish, given her waif face

with a summer tan, that I would have kidnapped her to the store
selling black boots and rhinestone waist chains. The store sold
blueberry-flavored smoking papers and T-shirts that read,

White trash in training, and *God created men because vibrators
don't mow the grass.* During another June, I wandered to happy hour
with my neighbor, who sold telephone book ads,

and after a car accident with a woman who rear-ended us,
and waitressed at a strip club, dusk made me feel strange, pouring beer
from a brown sack on the sidewalk, and air swirled around

the margarita joint we called "No Minors," a place where she later
reappeared, the tequila begged for Spanish, which became a night that felt
like running in a sauna, where she bought crack for $20 behind a Kroger

from a boy riding a bicycle. Dizzy, I watched my neighbor
find her an aluminum can, tucked her in the back seat,
then locked the doors and drove away.

I Know My Cat Is Responsible

for destroying my guitar. I lecture her
on respecting property, the proper conduct
of nighttime prowling, the pleasurable sound
a musical instrument could provide
when not engulfed in flames.

It's hard explaining to a cat why it is not
a good idea to knock over a lit candle
near a guitar. She knows that *no*
in an elevated tone means *bad*.
She will turn her tortoiseshell body
away and hide underneath a bed,
or begin her weak cackle at pigeons
behind a window.

Danger smells like a rogue rose.
At school, you help your buddy pull
the chair out behind Charles Singer,
the brat in choir, after singing
"Scarborough Fair," so you are suspended
for the day, then trudge home early explaining
to mother that stunt was not your idea.
You would rather sit in a trashcan.

Your job is no coral bliss.
My boss sends me to Brownsville
to start a new fire pump in an underground
parking garage. Water bursts into plumes
at street level after a pipe surge.
Danger is not my fault.

The winter bluish-grey outside is ashes.
All I wanted was to learn how to play
the guitar. Practicing the chords now,
if I could, would have been gloomy.

The guitar on fire sounded like a belt buckle
in a dryer. Mahogany set free as charcoal.
My flamed brain imagines
a cardboard, toilet-paper roll thrown
across the carpet. The cat paws it
as if pushing a hockey puck.

Shaken Not Stirred

You open your door. I remember the vodka
this time which made you smile
while shaking ice cubes and orange soda in my glass.
We sat in broken chairs eating chili.

This time which made you smile
you played Queen's "Bohemian Rhapsody" on the piano
after eating chili sitting in a broken chair
wearing a Metallica T-shirt.

You will tell me the orange soda contains formaldehyde,
and how you did a hundred pull-ups at the gym today
before wearing a Metallica T-shirt.
I doubt we'll ever be lovers,

yet doing a hundred pull-ups at the gym today
makes me want to rip your clothes off.
I still don't see us as lovers.
Finally, drinking too much, I needed to leave.

Ripping your clothes off
this time would have made you smile.
I needed to leave having drunk too much.
You open your door. I remember the vodka.

American Epic

We are not an unhappy couple

running along Peachtree Street to the church.

We say a little prayer where a car struck

Margaret Mitchell. We run past the white dogwoods,

the blue-black crows, up Heartbreak Hill at the hospital

while keys jangle in shoelaces. We want

a different narrative, one where we sleep on a train

only stopping for buffaloes. I admit my infidelities

in the dome car. I ignore you for vistas of empty fields

even if you wear a black, low-cut, velvet gown.

I suppose farmers and other military officers

will court you, but we survive on cucumber slices

and honey from a jam jar. You give birth to a son

I never love until I yank open the muslin curtains.

I run into the forest. I find a giant oak felled by lightning.

For the Best Outcome
           after Lorette C. Luzajic's painting, *The Best is Yet to Come*

I zoom in on the future 300%
to count eight rabbits stamped in
various positions inside red frames.

Nothing to do with a sexual appetite
if little rabbits feed habits.
Double-dollar figures

stand to the west strutting
their lucky bodies. No,
I do not bet. To improve

my outlook though, I want to
draw an angel fluttering above
with good health, beating wings

of common sense to the squatted rabbit
resting on her back. She is weird and pretty
spying Hello Kitty.

Wings flap, feathers,
still white and fragile,
would drop in a blink

and litter the splotched grass fields
where I want to sit, near bands of smoke
and scribbles of tumbleweed that roll on.

What's Surreal

Take me, I am the drug making your life surreal.
Pizza floats in your face. Businessmen in dark

overcoats. Heavy raindrops. Your grandmother's
necklace, the wired letter *G* kiln fired on metal,

gifted from you in a ruby Marshall Field's box.
Sleepwalking down Hyde Park Boulevard, dream

of driving off a bridge. Tillie, the ATM, says
nothing is left. Last spring's pot of tomato stalks

shot too fast against a stick. Years ago the bee
around a pomegranate seconds before the sting,

the sandbox, the wool blanket in a VW hatchback
at the drive-in movie theater. Take me, I caused

a cyst to travel up your spine—too many salt baths.
Why did you crawl in the bean field drunk

on Budweiser? Take me, I am the rose meditative
of your memory, remembering to float in water,

then a tide you navigate. Sunburned arms
and legs. Melting clocks and swarming ants

in the sand, your heart a white Frisbee thrown
from someone's hand.

Cilantro

I have seen their leaves glisten under mist.
Also, the aging rain forest of sprigs inside a bag

hidden in the refrigerator under the celery.
And plucked leaves laid bare on an omelet.

Other leaves were pinched into a ceramic bowl
with avocado and salsa for guacamole,

little angels, each I would call "Angelica."
Do some people say cilantro tastes soapy?

The latest sins washed out of the mouth.
You cannot smother a fire with cilantro.

Cilantro will not stop regret.
The recipe remains on a yellowed

index card, filed in the back of a grey plastic box
buried at the first Saturday flea market.

The recipe for how to say you're sorry.
How to stop crying. How to come back to the table.

Thursday Morning near Vancouver

I enjoy watching the woman don an exposure suit
before boarding the open-aired boat,
maybe excessive for a mild day at Granville Island
her hands stretching the suspenders over her shoulders,
and her left hand flipping her ponytailed hair
over the yellow hood, her right hand helping to clasp
the buckle in place around her waist before zippering
her pant leg. She rubs suntan lotion over her face,
closing her eyes, observing

progress later through her camera's zoom lens,
shutter button pressed over and over again
with her index finger after the purple-speckled back
of the grey whale surfaces in the harbor mouth.
His tail black underneath cuts the air, T-shaped

like a rudder. She sleeps at the stern, without earplugs,
despite the noise from the diesel engine taking her
and her husband from the strait, water furling
like cumulous clouds until the boat slows
down. She awakens, glances at, reaching
with a chorus of fingers to hold his neck.

The Trouble with Rowing a Boat Across a Pond
and Stopping to Embrace Your Lover
>
> after Maximilian Pirner's painting, *Lovers in Small Boat*
> (sometimes called *The Demon Love*)

Love is no duck soup—that boat tips over
when he shifts his balance.

Her powder blue and tan dress,
the commissioned one that took eons

to sew and will deflate into the reeds.
Then her hand will grasp the dock post

more desperately than his shoulder.
Is he a soldier that could not

wed anyway, for sex weakens,
the Romans said long ago?

So much easier now to drive
down the freeway to a sturdy lounge,

and deliver the black latex corset,
size *XS* from Etsy.

I might have won her over more
when she took a selfie with Snoopy

smiling on the gift bag. And how much better
to know the only water is at the bottom

of an ice bucket supporting a bottle
of Veuve Clicquot Rosé champagne?

No pestering yellow glow from a window
in the background or worrying

about spies behind any trees.
The waitress reserved the VIP booth

docked in plush red velvet with shutters
half-closed, the dimmer light bathing us

in marine blue and violet. No need
to ring St. Valentine, for this demon love

becomes a lemon dove with shiny horns
banging against my heart's thin hull.

Monologue of the Upside-Down Turtle
after Trudy Askew's painting, *Turtle Trainer*

Once, I fell off a plastic ball
and startled the trainer wearing
purple shorts over the grey earth.
I realized much later,
he broke from the routine

like dragonflies out of the wild
dying in swallow muck.
When the boy wailed,
I said I would hold two of us
above with my shell held
by the red-eyed mother shell.

I said, "I will put my claw, here,
on you and follow the webbing,
then you can put your claw
inside mine, you never know,
perhaps for eternity."

We are young with black speckles
and the yellow wholeness
of our bellies. At night, we looked out
from the bathtub. It was wrong
to have beach balls. Was it so wrong
to remember basking in marsh light,
or eating better than chopped meat?

We ate rotted lettuce and dried fruit
last Christmas. Took the laces away
from his boots in the closet.

The smallest turtle is staring,
wants to eat his white cotton shirt.

We love the patience of a snail.
The way the sun is
when I lift from water in early summer.

I will not forget our high balancing act.
We are bent clear for courage.
But the one held back by the boy's hand
is caught in a dark mouth like a minnow.

Emile Mourns with Her Daughter While Overlooking Paris
after Berthe Morisot's painting, *Woman and Child on a Balcony*

There Paule, see, be my little dancer.
Little dancer, see beyond the balcony.
The balcony will hold you up, in.
Up in pale blue-white, hair held back, light auburn.
Auburn-lit dance beyond the Seine.
The Seine draws help when you are down.
Down, my elbow resting. Umbrella for rain.
Rain, watercolored, not seen yet, above the yellow brush.
Brush your dreams beyond the golden dome.
Golden-domed Sacré-Coeur where we were
praying for your grandfather then.
He danced a little ballet before heaven.
Heaven is the last dance, Paule.
My little angel, never leave. There. Be.

Madame Maxwell

is a cat, charged in grey and black, ripe from next door
who prances through my backyard across the fence top,
as if she is a queen that rules, crawls underneath my deck,
urinates in the pea gravel, at her leisure, this air beneath,
reserved.

I drink Grey Goose martinis, smoke Marlboro Reds, smell
afterward, then realize a sick fantasy of you—my ex-wife.
She's a mini-Godzilla from you, or you, fifteen years later
(you'd roar at this), deciding to reincarnate pieces of your soul
as this furry demon-angel.

Now she, or you, appears lounging confidently on the hood
of my brand-new silver Tahoe. I squint, and she swallows
my white breath, descends, snapping hateful Kodak eyes.
Clawed paint, this could only mean it is you! Ah!

A moment to cherish! But why return now?
How I wanted to wear you like a gas mask.
Have you returned to ask if that Russian slut and the bologna
sandwiches cured me of your venom? Did you bury
yourself all these years in the damp earth only to resurrect
and fly my glider into the thermals?

You hissed when I tried an ammonia and soap concoction,
spray cans of cat repellent failed. Now I've spooned
onto a plate Fancy Feast Seafood Delight
mixed with Prestone and followed this version of you,
your feline movement towards a spreading chestnut tree,
eventually wobbly and knuckling.

Music Anti-Pantoum

Why did these songs come from the badlands,
        more broken and off-key than we have ever been?
Some of us are too ready to jerk the needle off.
How we wanted vinyl, just one 45 to stay alive
with a B-side. To rock.

More broken and off-key than we have been?
Some songs suffer from overplaying,
        moaning about their shelf life more than ours
in their worn boots staying alive with 45s on their sides.
They say enjoy each force applied to a load.

A sorry lot, those songs—why don't they karaoke at a bar
        or rock at the Mucky Duck?
They would enjoy each force applied to a load.
They coax us to throw wind in the back of our lungs.

We do not feel sorry about singing karaoke
        or rocking the Mucky Duck.
We sing those songs like pieces of flesh
thrown like a wind from the backs
        of our lungs after begging us.
We play music like it's DNA,
        like blood buried in the dirt.

One last chorus from the singer-songwriter. Swallow deep.
        Do not feel sorrow at the Mucky Duck.
Pocket your leftover dollars for the jukebox. Jam on.
Let the songs wind up.

Stockholm Syndrome

We are pale green moths in a bank vault.

He is an emergency God under fluorescent tubes.

He slices pears with a knife. He shares them with us.

I *mayday* the Prime Minister.

My pillow is a duffle bag of 90,000 Kronor.

I miss my pajamas.

We hum...*Kissing me softly.*

The robber brings a portable radio. It plays comfortable music.

Our watches should not have hands. Time crawls as fast as a crayfish.

The robber shows his true colors. His rouged cheeks.

He removes toy-store spectacles, a thick-brown wig, a reddish-brown mustache.

I cry that I cannot see my daughters.

They do not eat the leftover fish.

I am upset. Their dinner is meatloaf.

The robber places his arms around my shoulders.

We hold hands. I feel secure.

My children eat their dinner.

I tell the Prime Minister that I am willing to leave with the robber
in a blue Mustang. Real mustangs are better. No tracking devices.

The other hostages want to go with the robber too. It sounds stupid.

Teargas or angry bees—we do not know
what the police will drop in their drilled hole.

The robber asks if he can caress me, and I say, "Yes, yes you may."

What Follows Are Cuts for the Best Possible Revolution
after Steven Evans's art installation,
If I can't dance, it's not my revolution!

Track 1: The philosophy professor said if running is boring, just run faster

Track 2: I danced in the limelight

Track 3: I danced in early light without water, and drove down the road wrong

Track 4: I danced in dark light like a panther and wouldn't stop then I was toxic and smoke

Track 5: At the disco backed by neon, and silver and gold light, I pretend to rain again as a younger version, blooming like a remix only more bulletproof

Track 6: Before the remix, I sweated and said too much, "Goodbye"

Track 7: The revolution, a riot, doesn't matter if I can't dance

Track 8: The revolution as wild, no borders

Track 9: I punctured your revolution like an arrow

Track 10: Climbing up the mountain, my body is tainted, scrutinized, and quivering

Track 11: The mountain sliced by sunset, whispered by wings of a hawk

Track 12: I had many gaps, only constant craving, wanting more, more, and forward

Track 13: A life of telling your heart to press tilt, your beat, the red muscle to repair, whether this is beauty that's going on

Desire at No. 13, Calle Flor Baja
after Mariano Fortuny's painting, *Fantasy on Faust*

What shall we believe
of a piano planted inside a studio

next to a garden scene showing
Mephistopheles floating above,

dressed in a purple suit with a rooster
feather in his hat, his cape offset by

the low flight of a white owl,
one of the devil's emblems?

The flight that fantasy will take.
The flight path is a type of opaqueness,

more distracted, more fantastical.
The piano sounds strike innocence,

so we feel the deal Faust agreed to,
transformed as a musical evening,

one where we see the milky pages
splayed on the rouge floor reflecting

how we live, weighing us,
like what keys to play before time expires,

which urges me to want to see you now,
with a gardenia before you arise

from those bedsheets since morning threads
light, for the ivory in the eye.

The Joy of Wild Things

Musicians wrestle everywhere—
instruments not ready to be plucked.
Sound is a message sent to the galaxy
only wondering for a response.

Wild is alien. And alien is like keys
on a piano I never learned. Joy is I
don't have to worry about pianos, violins, guitars,
cellos, and drums. Joy is listening to a bad rehearsal.

Joy is an unbalanced chair and its wilderness.
Ivory for keys—less joy when I look at elephant tusks.
Wax to cast a head is joy. To touch permanence,
what was cut off, not deserving.

Joy is a fickle soul—to pay to see wax sculptures since you
did not live in France during the atrocities. Wild is the thing
inside like a baby. Unborn to living and when exactly
does living count?

Joy begins when wild opens the unhinged door.
When weeds in a pedestrian garden take over,
wrestling away the scent of a ginger lily.

The ginger lily dug up with your father using a dull shovel.
Plant holders not unscrewing from the stucco wall.
How does a screw get like that? Joy is walking away
from what I once loved. To pass along the planted pot.

Joy is color. Vermillion, crimson, and not knowing
what color is for the eye. Joy knows paint tubes
were born so Monet could paint outside. To be drawn
outside is wild.

To paint icy water and to touch ice crystals
is a chill—the wild brushstroke. The horsehair
for a paintbrush—shortened, cut, assembled, and wrestled
like strings for a wild act.

Van Gogh's Lover Poses at Le Tambourin Café

You brush with your narrow strokes. I drink beer,
light a cigarette for your canvas.
I sweep up my hair under a hat with red-feathered plumes.
I want to pose nude on the silk sheet of France.

My cigarette burns to see your canvas.
I wait for every parasol to open and smile at my polka-dotted,
        blue-black skirt.
I will pose nude for France's silk sheet
if only the geisha behind me will dance
        on this tambourine table and chairs.

I will open when every parasol smiles at my skirt.
I hope my café will never go broke.
The geisha want to dance on this tambourine table, these chairs.
Do you paint here for food or love, Vincent?

You can never have your paintings back if I go broke.
Don't paint me over a scraped-off woman.
I want you to paint for love, not meals.
No more beer. You brush your narrow strokes.

Drowning in Art

When You Are Drowning in Art

When you are drowning in art, I figure
as I draw the sheets closer in bed one night—
after finishing another story from David
Sedaris's book, *When You Are Engulfed
in Flames*—

the landlord of painted canvasses
that lives down the hallway
demands you pay admission
to see more exhibits where frames
buoy your weight around
events oiled with crowded lines.

Take Jasper Johns's *Corpse and Mirror II*
for example. The attempt is to evict
you into the ocean of yellow, blue,
and red-carpeted undertow.

Is there a rescue in the future?
Bobbing from one gallery to the next
is like smoking your best cigarette.

And when will photographs cease?
Diane Arbus's *Two Ladies at the Automat*
feeds you a theatrical image to shake
and remember as if you haven't eaten for days
unless you count the salt.

Besides submergence, you inhale
urges to copy what has already been done.
The ship yanking you from waters
of charcoal penciling,
more crosshatched pen & inks—
not to mention shadowboxed collages—
can't even locate the lighthouse.

Monologue of the Woman Who Builds a House of Cards
after Trudy Ashew's painting, *House of Cards*

The truth is we are trumped in a forgotten circus.
We travel from stations to tents of trickery
where we spring into our funny, ruffled costumes
fighting against sleep.

For this pose, we play with a powder blue deck of cards—
their corners almost round. This pyramid collapses
yet never will collapse. Our plain eyes
ready to act.

People club us with forgetfulness
until we say, "Pick a card, any card and place it
back in the deck." My daughter will spear
your selected card with a stare. The church

is clean in her heart. In this building, the only king
without a mustache is upside down as she wants.
She is not a half-girl. Her story is built on its slant,
her legs crossed in triumph. The men joke,

but they are not lamb-headed. I am
only a happy brown spider. Our circle game lives
in this wooden crate. When I pass the last card,
I want my suit so pure.

I Have Traveled
    after Emilio Boggio's painting, *Fin de la Jornada*

When the horse halted the wagon,
the parrot fell out.
The horse sniffed yellowing grass,
and the caged parrot toppled
onto the mud-caked road. I had not owned
the bird for very long.
Fragile and young, it sang a little
as I begged for fruit I suspected
women wheeled ahead in carts.
The horse gnawed grass blades, then lifted
its head to eye workers walking,
and "Venezuela," I cried standing,
always wanting to own a house,
not floating on a river like this,
but near a good market as the horse started to neigh.
"Oh yes," this precious land, a rifle shot could knock
an animal dead. Instantly. I imagine two lines,
crisscrossing from eyes to ears,
magnum point in slightly above
sweetly, gently, and then we could eat
for us, for the country. I will drive
my belongings, my sweat into the nation's head.
The sun-white river had a metallic taste.
The horse wanted to drink as she grunted
at the parrot, thin behind bars.

Esther from Lynn Nottage's *Intimate Apparel*

Dear,

I should have run his mouth through my Singer.
He was the deacon's son,
a Mulatto who dug in Panama, cut stone
to sleeve two oceans together. He wrote
me letters, paying ten
cents for the writing, fifteen
extra for fluffier language.

I wrote him back at the ten-cent rate
humming a rag
down Orchid Street, buying
imperial silk regular
like the iceman.
I sewed gabardine singing
the spirituals, found strength
in the hallelujah, in the glory
of Scottish wool.

After we married, we bedded on my quilt
hidden with my beauty parlor dream
until I ripped at the patches of savings
one night, believing his lies. He had
relations with Mayme, my piano-playing
friend with her robe always tattered,
who stuffed the money
in his smoking jacket. There were no
more illustration books of Valenciennes
lace, of gardenia ball corset.

Don't be like me at thirty-five.
I came to Manhattan tapping my foot
too long ago. The fabric from these docks,
those clients off 5th Avenue were the cloth
keeping me four yards together in magenta red.

I was a virgin then, a colored woman beaded
with too many hopes, and I have returned
to that rented flat wanting separate
lives again. I wrote this letter
fifty cents later, to you, hoping you exist,
great-granddaughter.

Caryl Churchill's *A Number*

I   Bernard (B2)

So, I'm him all over again.
This baby, this original died.
I'm a do-over from bits of hair,
skin, scrapings. This, someone,
was four, a son of yours. He's a first
killed in a car crash with my mother,
and you wanted him back. I'm not
a real one, just a copy. We can sue
the hospital. There are a number
of us, taken from my cells, the value
they're made from, they're robbed,
I'm damaged, my uniqueness lessened.
I figure, what, each thing or glob is worth
five, maybe ten thousand pounds? I'd like to
know one of them, at least meet any number.

II   Salter

You are real, a normal birth. Do you think
your birth wasn't normal if I wasn't your
father? I'm your father. I said your mother
was dead, she wasn't happy, sometimes she
wasn't unhappy. I did things that made her
unhappy. She did it under,
you know when they say trains are delayed
because a person is under a train?
The boy was four much later when he was
walking. He wasn't on the platform,
rather at a friend's house. We had friends.
You know I liked you. Remember when I
read you boring little books? There was that one
about an elephant at sea? With red trousers?
I could have done better. There were far better
books. Maybe we could sue. We need a solicitor.
The value of you, who knows, they belong to you,
stolen, these persons from you.

The Baseball Stadium at Union Station

Is a train hauling fake oranges?

Transpose imagery

with a dead painter like Cézanne.

The conductor frolics in France

painting fruit on white sheets

or rocks in the Park of Château Noir

while Cézanne,

in a fit of envy,

steers the train

over the tracks

killing Junction Jack.

A multilayered poem

no doubt. One about death,

and jealousy,

and art, or a triple

into the gap

of nothingness.

Gogol's Dream During His Pilgrimage of the Holy Land
after Viktor Gontarov's painting, *Gogol's Dream*

Mary is a mermaid cupping a white flower
above the sea I stand on.

My nervous heart is like a mad bell, clanging
awkward scarlet. Is her baby coming?

She stares away, silent. I am not wise
to wear paisley black pants—I deserve to drown.

Wind races windmills absurdly since Pushkin died.
I am the mysterious dwarf that will redeem Russia,

and no bribe will stop this dream because my writing
is a bible for my country. So blessed, this Holy earth,

leaving Mary as she is. I must never wake up
since I am fragile. I will resist any priest who says

to burn these pages. If I awaken, then I must eat.
Pour vodka down my throat when I am manic.

Tie hot loaves to my hips. Save these landowners
and serfs, their faces guide like maps, their souls

like pale horses I ride for. If I shall break apart, pray
for stars to appear. Oh, sweet Mary with child,

cup me in your grace if I am buried alive.

Swirl

The June night is cobalt blue and ultramarine.
The hope stars and a bottle-green cypress.
A view faces east from the asylum.
The soul to swirl.

Under a cypress, bottled hope.
Failure is iron bars, full of stars
      as big as Venus.
The soul swirls.
A moonlit town with a church steeple.

Failure is not filled with stars,
      never as far away as Venus.
There is a room: a butter-yellow bed,
      rust-seated chairs, pale violent walls.

Is the end to eat paint and drink turpentine?
The soul within is the body,
      trembling.

After Georgia O'Keeffe's *Black Cross with Stars and Blue*, 1929

She sees the cross during desert walks as midnight

spreads near Taos like a thin veil.

Those hills in the background go on

like seeing two miles of gray elephants.

To paint a cross close to a remote *morada*,

use layered oil, ground-up pigment from a clay bowl

burnt from dry air, lotion on fingertips.

She would chisel, wipe oily paint on a hand-stretched

canvas, hammered to a wooden frame.

The wood is *piñon*, sawed local, endangered.

She pegs black to remind us how dark

the world is. Not too big, just rich,

so we do not forget.

I Will Dance

after Henri Regnault's painting, *Salome*

I smirk today to celebrate my last seduction—
dancing at the banquet wearing a gold gown,

thinly veiled by silk. And if I shall dance again
on Herod's birthday like the motion of the sea

rolling back with mischievous clouds above Galilee,
will my mother send another request to behead

a man like John the Baptist, who said her marriage
was unlawful? I know you are proud, mother,

that I can entice these men by turning my body
endlessly in half circles. I miss the severed head

by the dagger I am ready to unsheathe.
For my next dance, no, instead I will ask for

more than a blood trail. I will want
half the kingdom. I am bent so far now,

exotic like an oriental chest,
and inside, a leopard purrs, ready to leap.

Drinking the Troubled Milk

Reading Murakami

In my *Wind-Up Bird Chronicle*, the lieutenant
is an engineer. That's why he carries secrets, grumbles
about upset conditions, tempers over a body's maximum
pressure. They fade into a picture of that abandoned
water well next door where the hanging house stood,
vacuumed of its whiteness—black gold, a blanket
of space. And the tomcat is my conscience gone
missing after trying to make sense of the world as if logic
were bits of smoked gouda. The engineer is sorry
he can't specify this pump. A vapor cloud ignites
and settles killing men in this refinery
who were going to die of cancer anyway. I sleep
at the bottom of the well, stoned and confused by narrowness
under a stampede of stars until Cameron Diaz enters.
She claws down the side. Her left shoulder is leopard fur.
Her cascading tongue is twice as long as the tongue
on that Rolling Stone CD. Her incisors are gold-plated.
Yet my narrative is time-warped. When Kafka creeps
on Murakami while he's stirring pasta sauce,
he whispers he knew a lieutenant in the desert
of Sake. Soldiers called him Sake Joe—who was later
transformed into a fly so he could escape the Chinese
before they could peel off his skin.
Murakami throws hot spaghetti at Kafka,
but he doesn't die until the broken neck of a Kirin
beer bottle twists into his nose. The glass is tipped
with elephant garlic minced by a sword. If that's not
bad enough, Murakami recasts Gregor into a man,
publishes the story in *The New Yorker*. Meanwhile,
the engineer is fired. He spies Help Wanted billboards
along the freeway while the level transmitter
on the vessel that stores his regret continues to alarm.
In the epilogue, the crude oil returns to the refineries' pipes.
The engineer leans over a drafting table with his stencils
and Mylar and invisible ink. Our minds are windows
with tangerine veils. We sit in our quiet wells.

Fate

Today at work, I don't know about the water. The sky
is acting like an indigo church. Flat-bottomed,
grey boats ride on trailers towed by emergency vehicles,
sirens yonking. Helicopters of Blackhawk or
Coast Guard rescue-type, their invisible wakes like ghosts.
Darkness is nearby; Mother Nature blocks roads in her angst.
Orange cars park on the street headed toward
Barker-Cypress. I drink knowing I'm safe
but Amy begins to inhabit my brain after she talks.
Her lips turn down as if pointing to specks on the carpet.
She arrives at the office in gym clothes with a brown,
plastic bag. I can do tragedy. Amy, from Lafayette,
who drives a silver Tercel, says the crawfish
here aren't as good, not even at Ragin Cajun
on Richmond. Amy, like a bird with her collarbone
that spreads wings from her throat bottom to
her shoulder ends. I'm in a cloudy vision now, covered
by khaki pants made from God-knows-where. Here
at the office, I navigate spreadsheets.
They are horses threatening to throw me off their backs,
always hard to ride when they are liars, delicious
in their deception relishing in unfriendliness.
Multi-phased liquid as pressurized hate.
It would be beautiful if Amy had her clothes.
It's quasi-death-like, the situation
of impossibility, the sheriff knocking
on her apartment door, only five minutes to pack.
We trap inside ourselves. Our bodies walk to the water
where the levee is about to burst. As if we were on leashes
and we were dogs. Mother Nature walking the dogs.

Conspiracy Theory

> If prose is a house, poetry is a man on fire running quite fast
> through it.
>> —Anne Carson

I do not mind running
but not down uneven stairs.
Fortunately, I wear my
fire-retardant pajamas while

writing a simile about a fire extinguisher
and an evergreen breath mint. Without
warning, flames leap from the carpet
like firecrackers. I like a bad simile

with firecrackers—they were taboo as a boy.
But I am a man now dropping my pen.
A notebook opens on the desk.
I know the bank wants

this house as part of the new agenda.
Seconds later, I smother
the flames with creamed-colored sheets
from the office futon. I do not hear any sirens.

And I do not know if the new government
would care about my patio chairs
next to the Christmas cactus that threatened
pink blossoms. Are these not tools

to contribute massive profits for the central
banks? Who knows what will happen next?
I want a fire extinguisher.
The black and white aerial photographs

show a pattern of burnt surroundings
every other Sunday on odd months.
I wrap a wet towel around my head. I see
their headquarters, the Denver International Airport,

and the southwest satellite office's strategy
in a sleepy neighborhood. Strange pizza joints.
Night-lit bridges run through, closed
to redecorate.

Nocturne: Contaminated
for a worker at the Hanford nuclear site

Tonight   moon garden   more silver than stars

Lying in bed I want to hold that moth banging in the lamp

A strong wind swept through earlier   scared my blood

to a hot mess   sheets scented vanilla and white soap

cool and useful   I'm a blind prophet driving a truck

Downstream   damned with dust   there is room for blindness

that is like silence   oh   for the gentle gentle love of birdsong

I sing its melody until   plutonium hits   then I keep singing

I'm a worrywart   overtaken   radiation wears

a hooded mask in the dark ready to decay the body

Have tiny particles   sprayed on with diluted fixative

been filtered in the streetlight? My knuckles are a city

Do not sleep here

Postcard from Akron, Ohio

Here in the bathtub,
water speaks of its slipperiness,
thin suds floating

and either the water dazzles skin
with help from a cloth
or else a yellow plastic duck

pitches in. Each pass
is a windshield wiper
on a VW hatchback.

In the backyard, the leaves,
these pyros, jockey for position—
mulch candidates, ready to

snuggle for a party.
When one sings a slight burst
of flame, the others huddle in suspicion

like record label companies
swarming, waiting for the fierce burn.
The smell of Goodyear tires

lit as if cinder, where Mr. Buntz,
the neighbor, always said to love Jesus
and keep your bowels open.

The smoky horizon is milk-hued.
Leaves submit a bright report
like firecrackers in a model airplane,

and every course, amber body—
how many escape,
have a visa to stay?

I Am Walking

> after Matthew Rackham Barnes's painting, *Noe Valley*

The moon's majestic hand paints
the sidewalk like a white scarf.
The row house wood
barricades the Pacific breeze
as cool as a ghost, smooth like stone
by the bay. I walk past the darkened
Worthington's drug store,
past each building on a street
that murmurs until someone plays
the trombone like a mad elephant.
I had marinated at a bar after working
at the Noe Theater. What is left
is this walk to my clean home,
but I'm as tired as a can of dripping paint.
The neon red is as luminous as sin.
Red is to blue as shade is
to the next bright window.
My bluish shoes remain ox-strong.
I imagine my wife staying up late
wrapped in candlelight,
reading a book until our baby cries.
I imagine this long day
then a little calmness like a lullaby.

Poem Folded into a Short Film and Offered to America
after Garrett Bradley's art installation, *American Rhapsody*

Where will the carousel take us

and when should we lick a Popsicle

Will you drink the troubled milk

and who else wants to

When will you be ready to leap

high enough to catch a balloon

When will you reveal

the pleasure of sugar cane

What does the tree say near the dirt road

Before getting up for this journey

how many revolving doors to be stuck by

How many white sheets shall engulf a traveler

If I fall asleep

imagine how long before

the radio quiets

When will the fire stop smoldering

and cool us enough to fly

as if to pilot a dream

The Puppet Show

I play anger bingo with Hound Dog.
He missed auditions, didn't make the cut
two years in a row. He smells victory
growling "I" statements without smashing
his guitar.

Al Gator won ovations squeaking
as a reporter in the Mr. Bush skit asking
jaw-trapping questions. He attacked
the horsy that rode in leveraging his tail
against a two-by-four. He curbs aggression
now by folding paper airplanes.

Lucky Ducky refuses to act like a ping-pong
ball. She doesn't bounce between two
ponds anymore. She channels waters in her
bathtub—newly Feng shui'd—despite
too much of the drinky-winky.

I stuff my helping hands around anxiety.
I breathe out color palettes of feelings
in front of the bathroom mirror. I script
the end—they reel me above on a fishing
line as the rulered curtains close
and the violet Christmas lights collapse.

Adam Bock's *The Receptionist*

What you say in the Northeast office
travels beyond pastry romance advice.
Behind Mr. Raymond's door, I feel
the tentacle of something unspeakable
squeezing what the company does
for clients. Aren't you the face
of this mission?
And why is your head not wrapped
around what headquarters does
when a meeting goes south? When
Mr. Dart visits and takes Mr. Raymond away,
why didn't you call his wife as he
requested? You say you don't have a wink,
but I thought you knew everything and if you
don't have the ring of things, then who can I
trust for voicemail or chocolate donuts
with sprinkles? Or maybe you'll only
remember when Mr. Dart takes *you* back
to Central. Maybe I'm extracted
because I was on your side, and yes,
I'm stapled next even though my desk
will look occupied. I'll never return,
we won't be replaced. No one will ever
cross this way, we won't escape
this hexed twilight we thought was normal.

Ghazal of Neil Gaiman's *Coraline* After Seeing the Movie

Oh, little Ms. Jones, how did you know to avoid the bad, bad buttons?
I wore 3D glasses, and the silver screen jutted the mad, sad buttons.
Mango milkshakes swiveled, poured like real from the chandelier.
A model train stops, wheels gravy near your other dad's buttons.
After dinner, you caught cotton candy puffed from cannons
before the mice circus began above the ghost lads' radical buttons.
And a black cat talked in this plane, this dream away from home?
He must have graduated a few lives before with ironclad buttons.
How did your other mother kidnap your boring parents, lock them
in a Detroit Zoo snow globe? You wouldn't stitch and add buttons.
So you made a deal, your eyes if you didn't find the eyes
of lost children before the crosshatched moon had buttoned.
And I, John, escaped from this theater, glasses disposed of. Snapdragons
bite, roosters pop caramel corn thanks to those horrible caladium buttons.

Jacob from Sara Gruen's *Water for Elephants*

Looking back, I marvel at surviving
the circus train set for Joliet
as a First of May. I don't know how
I avoided the jake
that gave Queenie the Jamaican ginger
paralysis. And I wasn't trampled after
the stampede with the elephant that understood
Polish and when we went broke, I wasn't redlined
off car 48 or the menagerie team.
I'm spiral cut. One vet exam
short, and all I wanted was a ride to Ithaca,
and if that meant endless wheel clicks
and playing cards with Kinko and Camel late
on burlap feed sacks with a lantern too low
on kerosene, then yeah. The harmonica
that played triple tunes were chords of my life,
songs I couldn't recognize and don't know
now. I was amazed as if they were pink sequins
on a costume Marlena wore, something
I could bank.

American Sonnet for My Cat

I do not see you lounging in a chair, certainly not caring
to pose for somebody, more like perching on top of a chair
near the bright yellow of a living room wall. I do not see navy blue
or carnation of your body, not part paint palette, not part base
of a floor lamp with light you would not want to be turned on.
I do not hear a bird song as soothing, more like an alarm
as you attempt to protect me from the blue futon position.
You are tortoiseshell, named Mardi Gras, but as a collage
of tan and dark. Throw-up heaved on the egg-yoked floor
is not unlike ambers of a campfire popping the night before
the mud locks in. We live in a two-story box, not as figures in
contrast, more like shapes hiding in a brown paper bag. The bones
of your escape. Outside is now your pleasure and nightmare.
It does not matter to love you. Trying to find you is not enough.

Monologue of the Creamed Camel
        after Jim Bones's photograph,
        Camels, We Were Here First Ft. Davis, Texas

How shall I not love the humans, nomads
that snap-shutter the Western Cordillera with a third eye?
They say the world is peeling off like whatever wallpaper is.
All I know is their sprawl is dead center

now in the grasslands. They dig for brushes
and cigarettes to honor us, riding with noble abandon,
not so sharp-edged. We appear ready to hump
in two directions without groaning.

Why would God allow them to follow us?
We love bearing their loads in transport
forty million years later since our ancestors
were bored in South Dakota like rabbits.

Could our Creator in her tipped joyfulness
match this grace as we ponder the Marfa Lights?
You will never capture my face so well as the guard hair,
the fat-laden bumps, and the serene proudness, headed

for the corners of earth's splendor.

Monolog Schmondolog
after Cary Leibowitz

It's not like or dislike it's how you figure this
stack of trashcans with me in a beige suit
helps my self-esteem because the smaller
cans are for liars and cheaters who don't move
as one in a season where there are two umbrellas
over sympathy instead of one but crying love
always leads to a bigger piece of the pie chart
to only hope there isn't a line or criticism when
I wear colorful clothes because they put up
and smile as a dinner date would if I ate
a plate of spaghetti and drank chocolate milk
from an official holder but not every hour will
end up happy more likely to waver between
blue sad and yellow sad jealousy doesn't help
either nor does sitting around all day eating
fried chicken does not make sadness any better
it is not worth copying me or meeting me on
an airplane like a friend of George Michael
I work for the candy apple escalator repair
company my self-esteem is less than a nickel
sadness is gritty but I love that you're funny
maybe the Tunnel of Love will help me
you could see me if I could love you more than
Michael Jackson I'm always hungry if I don't
get a flat tire you could be my hero

The Eating Season

is necessary.
Let us praise what matters most—
a serving of jalapeño stuffing,
brown gravy smothering arugula.

Ooh, during this time we eat comfort
like never before, slay pumpkins,
crack pecans for pie
until sunrays fall on frost
and cast serious doubt on any further movement—
consider those blessed hearts shut up on the eating season.

They schedule doctor visits
and jog even in bad weather.

They fret about chia seeds, omega 3s,
count steps on their fit chips,
power walk the multilevel parking garage.

They swallow health—
vitamins with purified water
rather than douse themselves in Bloody Marys.
The Cowboys play football on the outside TV
in front of sofas and rented heat lamps as the turkey deep-fries.

Let us hunt, those who must, for the eating season.
Let us recline and praise these days
in unison, leaf color turning from green to yellow,
as we hold hands ready to fall into the valley
of early darkness.

Gravy Matters

On the last day before the great flood
you can bet your quiet stars
this will flow
in a roast pan
after drippings stick,
flecks of road tar
on a run-over possum.
You can bet that celery rib
is broken to pieces,
that carrot stick
is famous like a white oak
without bark,
that onion minced
in a chopper is
six ways towards Sunday.
All browned and fragrant,
like a yellow rose
eked for your thin
heart's blessing.
Weathered from sandstone
and shale, dirt will keep
leftovers the way
it carries rain.
We will spade
through centuries
until we discover
each bent fork
rested in dried broth
and bay leaf.
You can bet gravy will return
heavy-bottomed, strained,
covering everything you remember.

Eating Right Because
        after found text from David Zinczenko's book,
        The Abs Diet, Rodale Inc., 2004

most diets are about losing.
The Abs Diet is about gaining.
The Abs Diet is based on the
simple notion that your body
is a living, breathing,
calorie-burning machine,
and that by keeping
your body's fat furnace
constantly stoked with lots
and lots of the right foods—
and this is important—
at the right time, you can
teach it to start burning off
your belly in no time. In fact,
this diet can help you burn
up to 12 pounds of fat—
from your belly first—
in 2 weeks or less.
And just look at
what you'll
gain in
return.

Yoga on the Roof

of my hotel room, pounding
on the cool terracotta
lined with painted wall tiles.
Underneath, I'm trying to sleep.
Two women, my friends, probably
raise their arms in sun salutation
surrounded by potted hydrangea,
then stoop to plank position,
barefoot or not, who knows,
that thud is as bad as the reverb
from the bells that rang earlier—
San Miguel is not a place to sleep now.

But, just two notches
below on the middle shelf
of my subconscious, the spot where
kindling is lit, a flame inside tropical,
banana-strawberry sensual, slippery
velvet blood, key lime pie muscularity
is stuck in such word registry: "yogurt"
is on the ceiling. Cartons of yogurt empty
on the floor, globs lather up high,
like hookers crashing a wedding party.
Yogurt plain, yogurt with fruit or granola.
Not once through childhood
did I eat yogurt. Maybe it
came from people who invented yoga
in a country that used an old alphabet,
or together were a custom practiced
while harvesting cultures, the first money
borrowed from a loan shark
who traded cows in Prussia
passed on to my grandparents in Ohio
to my parents, to me somehow.

The women are sweet and ingenious
in the way they walk to breakfast
with me on a narrow sidewalk
past the parochial bells that clang, clang, clang,
past the bitten-off corn speared on a wooden stick
lying on the cobbled street, past a god painted
on a taupe wall that tears your hunger
away with pleasure.

Secret Room

Antonia Teresa,
your place is comfortable with fire.
The bathroom window is caved in.
My safekeeping and dreams of trains
add ambiance except when roosters awaken.
I love pan dulce for breakfast,
Mexican quiche,
hypnotic wind in the towering cottonwood,
leaves that make sound rain.
I found the cool thickness of adobe walls,
heaven in your hammock,
bliss in flowers, hummingbirds,
I saw my first roadrunner.

Antonia Teresa,
eat at the Falling Star.
This is the last night of a honeymoon.
I'm fearful in your barrio.
Behind gates, your charm.
A 200-year-old stagecoach stop.

Antonia Teresa,
I want you to take me back next summer
to swim in your pool.
I'll paint waves, pink gowns,
indigo forecasts
in watercolor for this book
shaded next to your nightstand.

The Writer Who Drives a Taxicab

Passengers, you never see them
again. I write romance.
My eyes bulge when I hear from the backseat
what causes divorce or *what do women want*?
After a fare, I jot down the juiciest details
in my trusty notebook.

I wrote *The Platinum Key*—
strange how it's my biggest hit among Italian men.
Armand is a French soldier, a ghost
who discovers centuries later, his chérie in Minnesota
after she is struck by a thunderbolt.

From the notebook, the many fares,
I work on my latest book. A young woman finds
her way-older husband diving
in a swimming pool, then just
l'amour fou in a lounge chair with Byron,
the poet. What a buoyancy of spirits!

My high school sweetheart delivered
a typewriter, said, "You wanted to write.
Now write." Those early years living in Europe.
I saw the affairs of young women,
those senior husbands.

Driving to the airport or the Galleria is the best work.
Royalties now aren't much. This driven digital age.
You always wanted to write. Now I have typed,
kisses to my high-school love.

Don't tell my new boyfriend
I'm a seventy-five-year-old grandmother.
I won't see doctors, lawyers,
oil and gas executives again.
Inside this SUV, they romance the ride.